Come Out

Carrie LeeAnne

BookLeaf Publishing

India | USA | UK

Presentation by *BookLeaf Publishing*

Web: www.bookleafpub.com

E-mail: info@bookleafpub.com

ISBN: 9789358318036

First edition 2023

For my little witches, my daughters. I hope you'll never hesitate to come out, too.

ACKNOWLEDGEMENT

Thanks to the accusers for proving me to myself.

PREFACE

A witch is someone who is outspoken, who is odd or unordinary, who owns land and assets, who is deemed suspicious. A witch is weighed against a stack of Bibles. A witch has too many pets. A witch has had too many marriages. A witch talks to herself. She has odd dreams, mannerisms, birthmarks, and scars. A witch makes questionable choices. A witch doesn't bleed. A witch worships the moon. A witch wears a scarlet letter. A witch writes poetry.

*Like the moon, come out from behind the clouds.
Shine!*

-Gautama Buddha

*Three things cannot be long hidden: the sun, the
moon, and the truth.*

-Gautama Buddha

Wicked Good

Coming out as a witch means owning all of it.
Every emotion, your opinions and advices,
mistakes and regrets, the things you love and the
things you despise, the love that went wrong and
the love that went right, the things that make you
who you are.
You can't un-drown your sisters.
No amount of tears will snuff out the flames that
burned your mothers.
But for them, you can choose to live as freely,
now, as you can.
So tell their stories by telling your own, the best
and the worst of it.
Include the things you've torn by your own
hand, and the beauties you've created with those
same capable fingers.
Black is the presence of all colors, so wear them
all, however heavy the cloak.
Your shoulders are powerful and know what it is
to carry more than they should have to bear.
Do not fear the heavens you open yourself up
under.
The brim of your hat is wide enough to shelter
you from the criticisms that may rain down and

strong enough to hold the weight of what's
worth saving.
Your boots can tread this tangled path; your truth
will be your guiding light.
The night sky is your mirror, so stare into her
often.
She is you in all your complexity and bottomless
depth.
The stars are the glimmer of your brilliant heart
flickering with all that sets you apart.
And the moon is the brave in you, aglow in the
dark and leading you to move ever forward.
Once you step onto the path of knowing,
There's no going back into the broom closet of
the before.
So go on and come out, and do your best to
Be wicked good.

I Bought Dresses

Today, I bought dresses for
the skeletons in my closet
I just figured
if they've got to come out
they may as well look good
while they're at it
They're not the most modest
but they're sure to be honest
and honestly who could fault
a bunch of bones, dead and old,
for not fitting into anyone else's
mold

Writing

It's been written,
that words come down like lightning
and if not opened widely,
they fall within the small cracks
of our being,
and we only retrieve them
when we're crying.

My Heart An Ink Pot

I wrote a book in my head last night,
sat straight up in bed and bled
the words from my eyes,
my heart an ink pot spilling over
and out onto the seams of the sheets,
trembling from the tide of the pulses
of all the people I've come to leave,
deafening echoes of a shot that rang out
in a dream.
It sang of sorrows long-silenced,
good intentions that led to the
death of the freedom to intend
anything ever again, and my soul
ached as I sank,
ached as I sank
back to sleep.

Type-Written Fire

The ink: the lighter
type-written fire

Combustible medium, portable, device;
Ignite!
Made of mental metal, plastic plans
Head-filling flammable fluid
This pressure
This liquid
I am means to—
of—
ignition
Flaming, firework feelings
Ignite!

Don't blow smoke.
Don't blow smoke.

Don't blow smoke.

Hanging From My Heart

I'm out in the ether
Hanging from my heart
Sitting among the stars
Swinging into a constellation
In anticipation that you'll see
Something you recognize in me
And feel at home here in the dark
Somehow I hope I'll make a mark on you

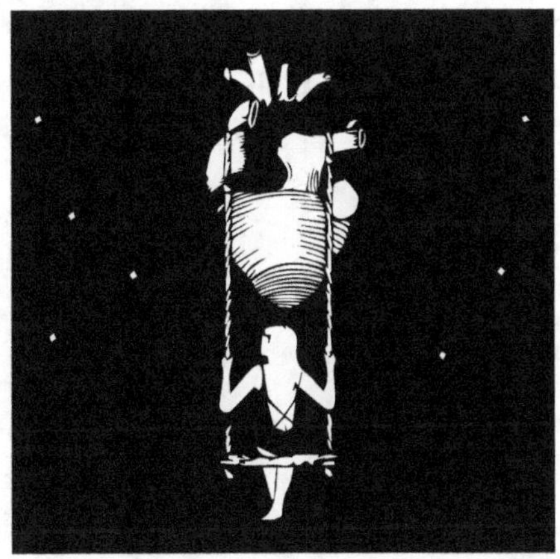

Mr. Beer Holder

You've grazed my shoulder;
I was just listening to the band,
Mr. Beer Holder,
liquid sex in hand.
I could two-step toward you
but cannot afford you—
the regrets for years.
They all think they're dancing,
bobbing like chickens.
We're bobbing nearer, gender victims,
beckoning for tears.
Mr. Beer Holder,
hold onto that hope in your hand.
I told you,
I'm just listening to the band.

Plays

I called it
like calling out plays
in a game
except the game was yours
and I didn't want to play it
My dad always told me "once a quitter,
always a quitter."
but I prefer not to be replaced
by any pitch-hitter
and I've also heard it said
that quitting while you're ahead
isn't the same as quitting,
so I'm waving you on
and sliding on home

Unraveling

You, there, are you sleeping?
Are you lying in your quilted bed?
Is the TV on to drown the sound of
my name inside your head?
Are you embroidered, too?
Have the threads of me and you
worn thin on your
patchwork skin?
I wonder, what will it take to
wake you, hold you, heal you, to
help you mend?
I wonder if it's worth saving, if
it's worth still wishing
you'd let me in, or if
we're unraveling
before we begin?

Since I Met You

Maybe it's the white-lit windows
Maybe it's this hurricane brain
The smoke plumes from an empty mouth
A stray dog hair on the quilt
The red inside the white wine
The clumsiness of intentions
Wishing the world would
stop my heart
I've missed you since I met you.
And I could go,
but I won't know where I'm going
until you get there.

The Fit of We

There's something in it
the fit of it
the arms that sit
atop shoulders
like armor
protective and
disarming
the face-off of toes
the tip-touching of noses
the closeness
the ghosts of exes and
regrets gone
when there's just you
in a room, with me,
and the fit of we.

Bound

The bounds of this love—
though little credibility or
ground on which to stand,
little proof to be supported,
it is pervasive & persevering,
severe in its haunting, pumping
through my veins, inside
my neck and eyes, my chest
and everywhere, inside
and through my body, so a part of me
that only my body's death could be
its death. It is achy,
cold & hot at once, shaky, burning,
wrenching. It screams and wails
for touch, for the tenderness
& the tallness of my love.

Sieged

It is sacred, what you do to me—awaken me!
Scarlet-lipped witch, Venusian beauty,
Magician to the stars that linger like violet
fingers
Deftly purging my violent sea
Plunging flavors along each crest
The savior of sweltering briny breast
Lingering
Linger with me in the evening
Play within me under your own brilliant light
Your silken shadow amused beside my dueling
depths
Undress the sky tonight and arrest the restless
waters
Pilfer the wreckage and keep the treasure for
your pleasure
Sultry seal, spin and squeal within and
underneath
Entreaty what you wish of me now and I will
bequeath
To you your wetted goddess crown as I come
Crashing into the truth of your wicked beauty
Reining in me divine
Stealing tension-ridden coral crimes with your
intellect and lines

Align yourself bare along what is under where
you can bloom
Along the bottom as my sole soul-shaman
An ethereal haunting, healing death at daunting
depths
As I become slowly still and break under your
will
Your wistful eyes the mirrored moons that
tranquilize,
The ocean, tempered tender, tips her fateful
tendrils toward you
Begging read, siege the sea,
Once careful cool drips seduced to dance as
warming peaks upon the beach
Only you, my blushing moon, can tame the tide
You are the grinning ivory Buddhahead, the light
under which I shine.

The Moment You Became Important

I can't recall the moment you became important
to me the way
I can't remember the day I was born.

There was You,
and there was I,
and there was a series of unalterable events,
and then: We were,
and how unalterable,
now: We are.

I watch while you sleep, and I think there must
have always been
a blanket of your sounds covering me.

Perhaps I had no ears before you spoke to them,

no eyes until you opened them,

no heart until you took the time to heal it,

and when they all awakened together,

there was You,

and there was I,
and there: We were,
important to each other,
though neither need remember
how or why.

I Wait With Them

You changed with the leaves as Fall
signaled to us all
the rushing in of a cruel winter
I missed the transition of this revision of you
your temperament hot then suddenly cold
a new mean you where lived the old
good man I know
as heaps of snow grow
outside and inside my heart the same
I blame the neglectful season
as the reason
you hold out your love like water
to the browning rooted stems
and I wait with them
so that my love for you
doesn't change too
into hate
feeding myself with the love I once

gave away
storing it into buried bulbs of hope
I wait with them
until the sun shows
through again

My Yellow You

My yellow you
drawn out in the bedroom
fractured half-mechanic in
white linen tomb
all yellow blue

bruising red the bedsheets
in my head, rolling
things I never told you
quietly patrolling
I blush green

we, two,
all hue
we
hew

This Scene

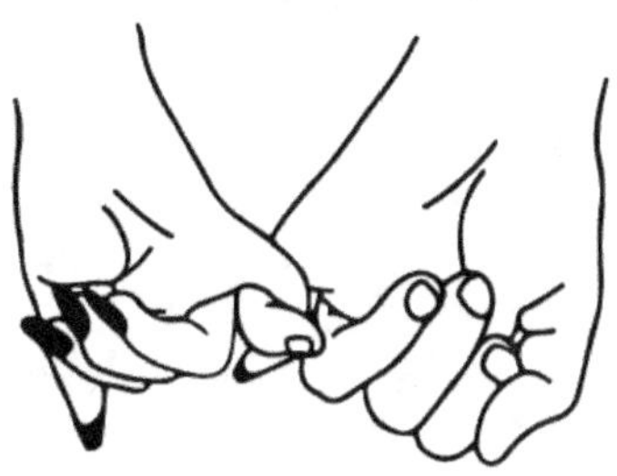

Put your things away, I guess
your laptop back to settle on the shy desk
your hat returns to tenant the shelf
sticking to me so
you aren't stuck with yourself
open my door for me, watch while I undress
listen to country blues while we cruise
(even a muse needs to be amused)
bouncing your head off your neck,
oppressively perfect
too silly but it's so cool
the ordinary things
that bring us back to
two, us, we
walking along with three hands,
deepest thank you to the trees that have
pulled the stars and placed them

within our reach
stamping bulbs of hope
on our memory
it isn't a camera, the mind
but some day
I'll replay this scene
all the time

Loving You

It is being in a wave on the ocean
with no footing, though there is
reaching, desperate stretching,
toward the safe landing
of sand.

It is thrashing about, being
violently thrown and battered by
rapids inside a floating device
too light & small.

It is a fight to the death of my inhale
by my exhale.

It is your own life's sabotage by
your own love's desire.

It's accidentally, involuntarily
assisted internal suicide.

It is the simultaneous soothing
and poisoning of a heroin hit.

It is the most satisfying self-harm.

Matchstick

if this is love to you
you might be a matchstick
careless haphazard fire starter
broken extinguisher pointing
ignited gasoline on a grassland
shard of glass on a delicate open
                    longing reaching gentle needing
hand

if this is love to you
your love is a hand grenade
in the sweaty palm
of a sadistic god

No Cake

Sometimes love
is like receiving
your birthday cake
with all the pieces
already gone

All hope
blown up in smoke
snuffed out with the wishes
that spent them
before you'd even dreamt them

The gifts given empty
wrapped in a bow
just for show and opened
quickly to be closed

All the planning
building anticipation
what was supposed to be
a celebration
ends instead in
devastation
but it's your party, and
you don't need
an invitation to cry
so cry if you want to

Ombre Day

Blue-orange ombre day
collapsing into Earth,
mountainous shadows jutting out
to prove Earth's worth,
competing with the sky's makeup.

It's as if she becomes shy, the sky,
realizing what she's up against,
allows retreating Sun to fade her
into a night of sorrow,
telling herself all the while
she'll try again tomorrow.

Who Is It For?

You licked the love
out of me
like a child with a cone
a prodding spoon
a hungry hunt
for drip and heap
of sticky sweet
It gets messy
remembering
who it's for—
the mouth, or
the mind?
Yours, or
Mine?

My Use

i know vices
enough to know
what i'm for
a rug placed over broken floor
tape on a tire hole
plastic covering cracked window
a distraction from the truth
i know
enough to know
my use

Clean Sheets

How commendable
of you to hold back
when it comes to live women
How courteous it is that
you keep your sack
in check, given the temptations
With all the breasts
and sexual suggestions
the flirtatious questions
ejaculated onto my rack
You'd think I'd be grateful that
you go off
to get off on
someone else
through a screen
you'd think
I wouldn't feel

this demeaned
that I'd realize
how forgivable it is
that you still
crawl into clean sheets
with me

Seedless

You were two-toned, un-straight
so I became
a rusted out watering can
wetting the crooked sidewalk
wasting my worth on
the seedless
still looking for
any sign
of life

Restless Rest

It's funny how we find our beds
only to find ourselves losing sleep
Our heads so full only now that our bodies are
empty
of energy, no life left, and we review our lives
left and right
Restless running after our mistakes while our
rest just runs away
Headed straight for daylight in a race with
insight moving against time
and tiring
finally
when the sun begins to rise

Night Mare

Darkness
Dependent
trots in
Relentless
bridled gait
braided mane
Night Mare.

Singed

Light is darker near you
and I haven't seen the way
for so many long and unlit days
You say,
"Where's the lighter, baby?"
And I say,
"I've lost it."
I mean: the way I've lost
so many other things
the keys, silly things, the
light inside me
I think, perhaps
it's in the ash
around us, or
what's left of us anymore
since you became
the narrow door on which
all hope is hinged
light is darker near you
I: irretrievably
singed.

I Don't Want to be the Bottle

I don't want to be the bottle
you place your lips to when
you're losing your grip again

I don't want to be the glass
whose transparency clouds your
ability to see through yourself before
you slip again

I don't want to be the reason
you lay freezing at the bottom
of the cup among the other cubes
of your cold self-loathing

I don't want to be the face
you see in the golden sea
you've set your mind
to sleep inside

I don't want to be an ally to your dictraitorship,
so
if you're set on drowning
keep me out of it.

Debris Not Yet Dead

I was afraid of everything
Everything missable
myself as dismissible
the preliminary post-traumas
of us

Across our fault lines
we still touch
ignorant of
our geography

I can't help but feel it first
(before there are words)
the rumbling of ancient debris
the crumbling of you away from me

It's in the eyes,
a stranger's or

the mirror's mine, in
his begging where yours isn't,
in a friend's visit after the funeral
of the me that died
beside your ghost not yet dead.

Cotton Rounds

I never have the right words
until he learns
he has the right
to lose his ears.

yesterday, I said nothing
of consequence—or everything
today, I say what I can
to make sense
of anything

my tomorrows are the stale snack
I cannot bear to place on
his hungry tongue

the hurt we hum
when memories come

my sewn mouth reaching out
to pull down the cotton rounds
shoved into the heart in you

you're the pipe-dream
I'm still chasing
even as you're erasing me
from your memory

she's your unrequited love
and you're mine.

Full of Empty

I cannot sleep
and I cannot eat
too full of thinking
of how you
emptied me out
again
the cost of it is undiluted
the taste of it is unsuited
for a tongue left
tender with the
surrendered taste
of you

A Hungry Monster

Whatever monster we feed will grow.

I took a brave bite of you
while you only
tentatively nibbled on me

*You took me for one to swallow when I am one
to taste.
There is so much more of me to taste.*

I listened while you spoke.
I opened as you closed.
I gave grace where you placed blame
in your same old coward way.

Now my love has grown into

a hungry monster.

I stopped giving her bites
to make her die,
but it's too late . . .

she's awake, and

she's turned on me, and

she's eating me alive.

And the more there is of her
(the more there is of you)
the less there is of me
left to eat.

Magnanimous Bird

Magnanimous bird
beautiful as blooms
flowering
losing petals
where bruises should not be
red and white
swelling skin
as thin as light at night
magnanimous bird
Have you not heard?
Love is not a privilege.
Love is a right.

Claymore

I'm used to sending signals
into the dark
I know the unpredictability
of ticking bombs
the carnage of relationship
grenades gone off

you were a minefield
of claymore

trip of trigger
intended
to end it

and it did

and I'm still here

alive.

A Guess

I guess you brought out the freedom in me
the exploring of it and the exploration of myself

I guess you made me into a woman with
a guttural laugh echoing out of the walls
of what had been an empty cell

I guess you gave me an altar on which
to finally rest
my interests, fears, fulfillments, creations
my losses and my gains

I guess you gave me everything
and I can't begin to guess
when the day came that I felt I had to guess
how you felt, and why, with all we had, I ached
bereft

I guess that's why I left.

That'll Do

If I could be important enough
close enough to you
for you to hurt me
that would be
enough.

You said,
"I might be in love with you."
I said,
"That'll do."

I opened the door
and held it open for you.
You left the room,
and I left the door
open
still hoping
you would walk
back
through.

Now the clock pokes
my peace of mind
with reminders of you,
each letter of your name

clicked out in the refrain
of her ticks, her cues
to move out of the hours she's passed
and into the future at last
without you.

So I'm turning the page on you
the way readers do
ready to lose myself
day by day
in the new.

Eclipse

If I'm the moon,
we must be the eclipse.
You loved me until
our lips touched.
Then, crossing paths,
we turned to black.
Now there's nothing left
to go back and undo.
You only glow when
I'm not over you.

My Things

Thank you for giving me back my things.

They'd been important to me until,
among our collective mess,
I left them in places I came to forget;

Dignity divided into scatters inside
the dresser drawers,
self-expression left shattered, swept into
the cracks on the floor,
my passion, my courage, my laughter, and fun
among the parts of me come undone;

I was bereft of anything left to lose
until I lost you.

Thank you for giving me back my things.

An Echo

I thought you should know that
when you go,
you will leave something behind.
I've been through this before
(more than a few times).
You probably won't want to take it back.
It will be deep and wide and black.
My friends will do their best
to mend it, sewing
sweet words along
the seams, and it will seem
to grow closed.
I'll be told to
leave it alone.
I'll be told that
if I don't, it will bleed.
In secret,
in lonely moments,
I will pull at the stitches, and I will
listen as it twitches a rhythm,
an echo of us.
I will let the healing recede.
I will let you bleed back into me,
just a bit,
in lonely moments,
knowing you don't want to take it back.
I thought you should know.

Following the Road Down

I should have taken the alley-roads, the
backroads, any other road but the one I took
today.

I could have told you what would come of it,
every tire-borne pit, every cigarette stubbed out
along the way.

I played those old songs—-the scream-speaking
ones—
that make me feel softer because they're all
hard.

There are a lot of ways I could have gone today,
but
you still wouldn't be very far.

I thought of girls' names and our tireless games
and all we had that wasn't enough.

I whispered worn-out words to the stranded
herds of our memories of what we called 'love.'

I cursed the stars, and her, our old bars and your
shirts

I'd steal but didn't keep.

If I could appeal to you now, I'd wrap myself
around you like a fender to a tree.

I shouldn't care to send you light and love, and I
wish to God I wouldn't, but my pulse still plays
a tune of us long after I learned you couldn't.

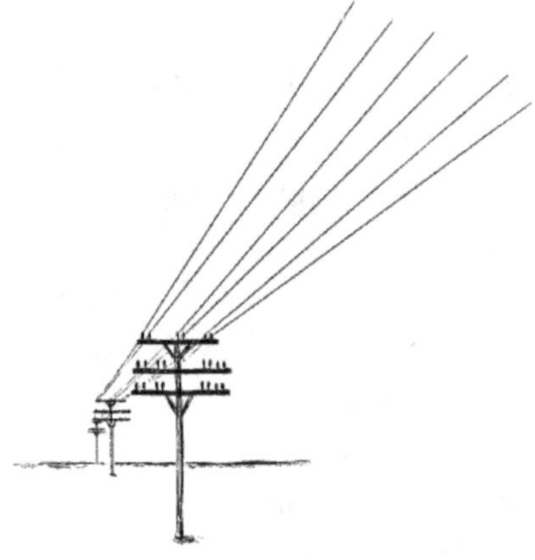

A List of the Ways I Remember You:

-when I wear the necklace you gave me,
    I remember that
    you really were trying
-people say your name every day, all the time
-when I look at our pet, I remember how much
    of a father you were
    and weren't
-when I found the ornament I'd bought for you;
    I'd just been wondering where it had gone
-when I'm chain-smoking in a bar
-when I see a car like yours
-when I smoke (it's a wonder I do anymore)
-people talk about narcissism all the time
-when my love shows me love, I think of how
        you couldn't,
        and how you tried to,
        and how you did,
        and how you wanted to,
        and how it was sometimes enough
        but not enough times enough,
        and how I needed it,
        and how I wanted it from you,
        and how he can,
        and he does,

and how maybe she does for you,
and how maybe, now, for her, you
finally do, too.

Use Him Up

I heard you say it,
as I cleaved to him
in my reprieve of you,
"Use him up, baby,"
and I did, didn't I?
With only the uselessness
of a remorser's cry,
it had been there, and
when I opened my eyes,
it was done, and I
had done it.
Calluses shorn now,
(at least I can say
they've been torn away)
I think, today, of your foresight.
How could you have known?
I think of your sin,
and, under my skin, the bruises
and wonder what uses
you'd had for me, wonder
if, then, before there was him,
you'd somehow heard me say it,
"Use me up, baby," else,
How could you have known?
Don't we only do what

we've been used to?
Don't we tend to use
when we've been
used, too? Else,
How could you have known?

Bitter Bits

Torrenting
bitter bits
my memories
habits
losses and pain
(what is it if not a typhoon)
my collection of you
flooding
running
from my bloated brain
like rain
to
a
drain

A Spiral is:

-listlessness
-wine at 1 o'clock
-avoidance
-picking up old habits
      right where they left off
-playing a single song 100 times
-refusing to cry
-crying anyway
-cursing the day it happened
-driving around in graveyards
       instead of going
         to the one at home
-smoking to get stoned
-sitting in the middle of
      the liquor aisle alone
-buying three bottles
-bottling it up
-feeling like there's never
      enough in the cup
-anything to rebel
-hell
-making the same mistakes
      of the past and telling yourself
        it's not that bad
-legs not working

-heart still hurting
-regretfulness
-senselessness
-impatience
-This.

Mirror Mirror

I'd like to speak to
the man in the mirror
the one that has made
a woman fear herself and
stash her self-worth on
the shelf and pluck
from her wardrobe of shame
an indifference to wear
herself thin
again and again
painting on silky
grin after grin
plunging out plastic perfection
disguising self-doubt with
pins in her hair and spray-on
self-loathing, betrothing
an "insight" into a woman's
worth,
we call it empowerment
we call it feminine and pretty
to be a slave to the
chiseled expectations
while our hearts are
held prisoner to the
mirror mirror on the wall

telling us she–no, you–no, me–
is fairest just to turn us all
against each other, set on
a quest to elude the mother
in us that tells us it's
futile to be anything
other than what we're
meant to be, the mirror
tells us our destiny is
only external beauty
in an armor of the sexy
that it's somehow noble
to tempt with extensions,
plumps, silicones and pumps
wielding swords of
distrust for our sisters
serving as modern maidens
to any misters that
tilt their instinctual
caps, look at the havoc
we don't see when
the girl becomes trapped
and the seductress set free
when we
only hone the habits of the
mirror mirror on the wall, now
we're the frailest, one and
all

Among the Changes

It's been so long since I last wrote.
You took that from me, among all the changes.
I'm still changing, or maybe it's everything else
changing
and I'm the only one still still.
Now I'm strong-willed, or lacking will,
or the ability to decide on one or the other, on
anything.
I keep losing things, or losing me, or losing my
mind,
if it hasn't already happened the way we lose
things over time.
I may slip into that now and lose this thought,
or this and that, whatever they may be, if I
haven't already lost them, or they me.
I'm in the habit of it, and it's nice to have it, the
habit, I mean,
as I'm in the habit, it seems, of not having
anything,
at least not so long that I don't lose it,
the way I lost my writing, or it was taken, the
way you took it,
or the way I was taken from you,
or the way it lost me like I lost you,
and all the other things I've come to lose.

It's been so long since I last saw you, among all
the changes.

The Void

let me just say this

to the void
that expands itself between us now:

> i am okay
> we are okay
> i understand, and

my care for you still waits
on the
 s u s p e n s i o n   b r i d g e
of our old love, suspended in time

until next time,

Sending You Light

I want to weigh on your mind
like you've been on mine
so I'm sending you light
and the idea that you might
die without me.

In Time

If there's a fight
between you
just wait:
people's vibes
don't always align,
makes it hard
to relate, but in time
(keep your peace of mind)
it can change,
just wait.

I Could Find An Answer

I could find an answer for anything.
Give me your options, and I'll give you
the whys and the why nots,
the pros and the cons.
I'll find it in the surroundings,
in the smallest things you wouldn't
have thought to see.
Take this flower pot, with its
leaning plant, and I'll tell you to
lean this way or that.
Tell me you're tangled up in
something tough, and I'll lead you to the
kind of fingers that untie those kinds of
knots. If you tell me you're weighed down,
I'll look around and find
a stream of smoke sagging out from inside

someone else's mouth and tell you
to breathe it out and
breathe in whatever is clean.
I could find an answer for anything.

We Were Beautiful

I time-traveled
to find the forsaken
future with you
as it unraveled.

I am breath-taken.

We were beautiful.

Now, there is distance,
and there is time,
and there are new lives—
yours, now. And mine.
But once,
before and still
(and with your will)

there was us.

The Tattoo Tells the Story

We who have ink
We all are writers
Our stories engraved in borrowed pen
By a hired scribe
All along our tired skin
An honorable grave to the
Sins, memories, wins, symphonies of the
Dust we've left behind us
And the hopes we hold within

Does She

Does she know I got you ready for the baby
I wanted that you had with her?
Does she know you still have me while she's
holding on to you?
I play house in my home like I'm the wife in
yours, but the apron is too small, because I'm
too big with what's wrong,
and I still smoke because I miss the inhale you'd
take just before you drug me along.

Like A Bullet

You think you left
But you still live here
In my head
Between my mind and
The time that has passed by
Nestled like
A BB gun bullet
Aimed years ago that
Took hold never to
let me go unscathed again
Marked then, you were
The perfect marksmen
So that I don't grow without you
I only grow around you
Your crime was a kind one
The plot still undone
Hidden in my mind
All this time where

No one knew where
It had gone
It is here
Laid to rest in the heart of you
That still lives on in the mind of me.

Forget to Forget You

He's good to me.
He knows I need reassurances,
so he gives them with no
hesitation or questions asked.
He's a great communicator.
He does the dishes,
goes to work, works out.
He hears me—really listens.
He's handsome and strong,
responsible and kind,
and I remind myself
of these and other things
when I begin to forget to forget you.
He's on my mind
all the time.

New Girl

You're welcome,
though I should be thanking you
for taking on a task after I'd decided I was
through
for trying to find the best that man can't offer
you
when I couldn't be bothered any longer to
I can only say I hope he makes you stronger
the way he made me find the strength to leave
New girl, I see you, and I see you seeming to
believe
that it's worth your maybe one and only life
to live it under your lover's un-bladed knife
I hope you know it's okay to decide
to leave, too, when it's your time.

Caverns

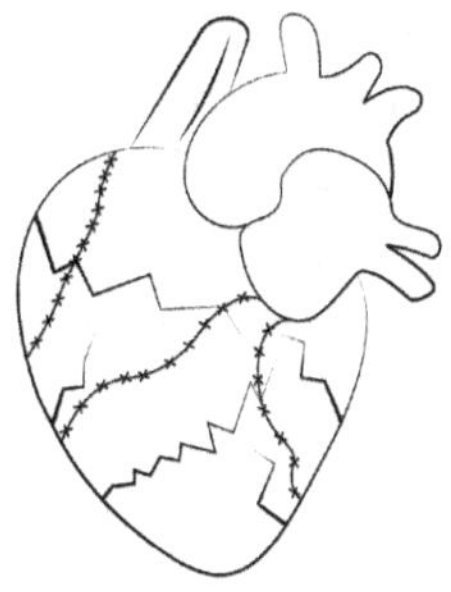

I would like to touch
the inside of my heart
and feel around a while
until I feel my feet settle
on one of its walls
and make a home there
where I should have been
all along
and start a conversation
and find the location
of every hole
and the origin
of every dark passage
and close them up somehow
and fill up the caverns
with something worth loving
and mediate the messages

that have been pushing
and shoving for so long
that have been breaking
off chips of the mortar
that have been necessitating
this slow sad murder
and clear it all away
I would like to feel as though
it's the kind of place
I might like to stay

When the Heart is Broken

When the heart is broken
—the chest cracked open—
we can see it as a death or
we can see it as a window
where there once was a wall,
and the thing about windows is
at some point, they all
let the light in
if only we
withdraw the curtain.

Call It Winter

Sun, with
her highlighter pen
brightening the light within
a feeling so far removed
I can taste it but
can't recall the food
see it building but
can't label the tools used
watch the trees bolden
more golden stripped bare
sense myself washed by her hands
as white as the strands
of her hair
stare into the soles of prints
left along
the surface of her skin
hear the echoes of
footsteps traveling the rim
of my own soul cleansed
as she selects each deadness
and carries it away
I feel her say my name
I breathe from her chest
feel death of a burden unearthed
see the change in the weather

        my own, my inner
call it Winter
but can't remember
what sent her and
why it is I feel at home
when she makes me cry
out to Fall
        my inner, my own

Pet

You were sent down from the soul-realm
To live inside this body just for me

Taking in the best I give and the worst I try to
hide a comfort and fur-laden sagelike guide

That's why when I look in and through your
eyes, I see so much more than just a creature

I feel you teaching me to grasp life less
intensely, a vision of the love you lend out
generously

Following around on lowly ground to look up
to the towering height of a species that
could cower at the power you have
to take hold of a heart

I had no hope to get mine back
lost from the start to you in your loyal gaze

My most faithful friend, my seer
your quirks, our mishaps, my tears

You leave, still I recall your help for years

My days are never lonely
since the day you came to own me

Hands So Worn

I'd never seen hands so worn as his
One middle finger wider than the others
from the time he'd slipped and made it
into a nail
Always with a project, be it building
or the brewing of wine
Some ball sport in the background
or news from time to time
When we were full up of eating
a disposal went unneeded
The same fingers would hold
a hand of cards, a basketball, a kitten
a mit in the same shade of leather
When we'd wake up we'd look to him
for the forecast of the weather
Be him sunny, laughter reigned
Were he angry, we'd take to the shade
of our mother, huddling together
until his clouded eyes squinted back
into the laugh lines we so loved
and wait for tears pooling lightly
that he'd pour over the plants he tended
somehow mending our hearts the same
Attending every game, competition
his middle name, but

avoid from him the spat
of a saintly or civic at-bat
No need to wear a hard hat
with a head as hard as that, and
back so broad there's no
sparing the rod, there's no
patriarchal rose without thorn
with hands like those, with
hands so worn

A Mama

I don't know all mamas
I only know mine
I know she's of the kind
With the kindest of hearts
Forgiveness that extends
Across time and transcends
Any transgression
She's taught me lessons in
Patience and love
To see that the best is yet to come
That shame doesn't live where
Tenderness does
And she taught me to write
When a voice won't be heard
To smile through the absurd
To compete and lose well
To leave pride on the shelf
To say what needs said
To cure a worried head
I don't know all mamas
I only know mine and
I'd choose a mama like her
everytime

When I Hear My Daughter Cry

When I hear my daughter cry,
I see Earth stoop to
Her haunches, watch as everything
She touches turns
to stone. I see Her
slipping off Her
spectacles, squint
Her eyes and
tip
Her
toes,
still Her breath—
and quiet every
creaking-tired bone. When rivers
ripple through bluest eyes, I know
Earth's pools have all run dry; I know
She listens with me
when I hear
my good girl cry.

Little Girl

Little girl, you test me
Aggressive from the moment you left me
Your graying tooth the dying proof of
The fear you forgot to absorb in my womb

When I showed up at work with a bloody lip,
and I told them the truth of who'd given it
They hardly believed the fiery free spirited little
beautiful beast you'd been born to be

I look at you, shrouded in wild golden mane
A reflection of the parts of me I'd left untamed
And I can't help but thank the universe all the
same
For granting me the honor of giving you your
name

It reminds me of your sweetness, all nuttiness
aside
The impish grins that sprout beneath spritely
eyes
You won't settle for less than to keep me alive
Only innocence in your dissonance,
my lovely little girl

Hymn

You sing
harmony
to my standard.
The way some sound unholy,
and others, unlucky,
using the same
machine, it's music when
you sing.

A Lovely Crash

There is a crash site
Where our clashing interests collide
Politics yours
Poetry mine
Videos enacted
My reading distracted
But your love
And my love
Get along just fine

Handyman Special

I've been a handyman special all my life
The first man to wield the knife
carved out a square
in the side of me that
used to be kind
And the next one took to the other guy's
self-made mine
and cut out his own
taking a hearty bite
the size of a small child
leaving behind a window
to the wildest parts of a girl
trapped in a tilt-a-whirl of grief, then
a few noblemen strutted in
setting out to neaten up
the gore of the gutted heart
underestimating they'd no idea
where to start, and, defeated,
fell to their knees
But oh my relief
when you walked onto the scene
and saw the potential of the jutting debris
as a stairway you could climb
all the way
up the precipitous ladder

to look a fixer-upper in the eyes
a quest you took to find
the woman you knew somehow
still lived inside
a vision you brought to life
not by your own hands
but by showing me
I was strong enough all along
to use mine.

Holding Space

It's my duty to
hold space for you
give grace
imagine places anew
come into
the darkness with you
take your hand
and guide you to
the light I know
resides in you
when you're
tired, scared,
doubtful, unaware
and spending your last dime of hope
it's my only hope that if you
come in a slave, you'll
walk out a soul
a little lighter

more a fighter
and seeing all the love you're worth
for what it's worth
it's an honor to
hold space for you

The Letter A

They marked her with it because they
couldn't see the one they wore themselves
made sure to decorate it with elaboration
so she'd stand out, and she did, though
not for what they'd intended
She took the shame and claimed it to make her
Able
not once pointing out that
the same letter
lives in the word Accusers, too.
It just so happens to be that she
looks very good in red.

Call Me A Witch

Call me a witch
    and I'll call you right

Ask me what I know of
    the wilderness at night

I know it bleeds black,
    just like my soul
    and the cat on my lap

Winter shrinking,
    spring small

Summer awakens
    the promise of fall

As hard as you hit me
    your stones meant to maul
    I can only grow, and I only grow tall

So call me a sorceress,
    enchantress, a hag
    for the crystals and cards I keep in my
    bag

Throw your Good Books at me
        I've got verses too

I can trust in the Mother and
        the Universe's voodoo

Can't you trust the one *you* pray to
        even with Satan herself (!) so near to
        you?

Call me a witch, go on,
        but whatever you do

Make it quick,
        I'm in the thick of casting
        a hexing spell on you